Amazon FBA

Amazon FBA Guide: The Best 8 Step Blueprint to get Started Selling on Amazon & Build a Six- Figure Passive Income Stream Business. (Amazon FBA, Amazon Empire, Passive Income, Private Label)

Table of Contents

Introduction

Fulfillment by Amazon is becoming a more popular business model for those who don't have a lot of capital to invest in a business right away. It allows those who are of the average income dive into the world of becoming a business owner without having to spend their life's savings. But there are still many people who don't know what Fulfillment by Amazon is, or how they can even get started.

This book is going to explain how you can get started with Amazon's fulfillment program, but more importantly, it will describe how to find a winning product to sell, as well as how to expand your business once it takes off.

I hope you enjoy the information you find in this book!

Chapter One – What exactly is Fulfillment by Amazon?

You most likely know the basics about Fulfillment by Amazon, but let's just recap what it is so that you understand what it is you will be exploring in this book.

Basically, there are two methods to selling on Amazon. There are direct sales, and then there are indirect sales. A direct seller is someone who lists items on Amazon, and then they handle the customer service and the shipping of the products. When you sell directly, you are in charge of shipping the item and handling packing, returns, customs, and anything else that's required to get the item to the customer.

Indirect sellers are those who store their items in a warehouse or fulfillment center that's owned and operated by Amazon. When someone orders one of these items, Amazon employees at the warehouse pack the item, ship it and handle any returns of the item. The advantage of indirect sales is that Amazon handles the shipping, customer service, and returns of any items.

Fulfillment by Amazon lets small sellers in some countries, including the United Kingdom and the United States, take advantage of this amazing service. Sellers of any size can ship items to these fulfillment centers and turn the customer service completely over to Amazon.

So how can this help you?

The potential advantages of becoming an FBA seller are endless. An individual or small business can utilize Amazon's customer service department, which is a large corporation. You don't have to handle the frustration that comes along with customer service, and you get to pay more attention to the products you're offering, as well as expanding your business.

Sellers are also spared the hassle of having to worry about packing, shipping, returns, and running to the post office, as well as many other distractions that come along with selling products directly. Another hassle that's eliminated is the need to rent or purchase any warehouse space and storage space for products, which can become very expensive very quickly.

So what about the disadvantages of using FBA?

The largest disadvantage is cost, which can become considerable depending on what you're selling and how many items you're storing at the warehouse. Amazon will charge around $1.48 a pound per packed item and an additional sixty cents to store that item. Costs for larger items will be higher, and the fees are greater, such as labeling, which can cost around twenty cents.

Another disadvantage is how Amazon holds money from sales in escrow for fourteen days to cover the cost of a potential return. Basically, this means you don't receive the money from the sale for around two weeks.

As with other services, any fees with FBA are taken out of your final sale price before you're paid. This can considerably reduce profits or eliminate them entirely if you don't choose a product that has a high enough profit margin.

Shipping can be another complication because Amazon charges you to ship to the fulfillment center, and then they can add shipping charges to final products. However, FBA users will qualify for certain free shipping credits, which can cut your costs down.

However, products sold through FBA are eligible for other Amazon services, such as Amazon Prime, which gives customers free two-day shipping and upgrades through Amazon Associates. This can lead to even more sales!

Another interesting advantage is that items shipped from a fulfillment center have Amazon packaging on them, which associates your products with one of the most popular and trusted brands on the planet.

So is selling through Fulfillment by Amazon worth it? Definitely!

Now that you know the advantages let's look at what you have to do before you even open up an account.

Chapter Two – What You Need to Do before You Open an Account

The requirements listed in this chapter are very important for success, and it's highly recommended that the product you plan on selling has most, if not all, of the requirements that are listed in this chapter. These requirements are a compiled list of tips for success from many different, successful, FBA sellers. They make anywhere from five thousand dollars, all the way up to ten thousand dollars a month using these guidelines.

#1 The Average Product Sale Price Should Be Between $10 and $50

This selling price of products on Amazon is extremely important to know, and it's something that you need to know before you place an order with a manufacturer. The ten to fifty dollar price range is the sweet spot with pricing because people tend to make impulse buying decisions for products in this price range.

Most people are not going to need any further research to make a purchasing decision because it's a low enough price that they will risk losing the small amount of money if the product isn't any good.

To further explain this, think about how much research time is spent before you make a large purchase on a new mower or a new television. People do not want to make an impulse buy when they are purchasing these items because they cost so much, and that's why you want to keep your product selling price within this range.

Another reason you want to keep your product sin this selling range is due to a lot of the products in this range being simple products that don't have a lot to them. For example, think about a mouse pad. It's a simple product with a low price, and compare this mouse pad to a radio. This is an intricate product with a lot of moving parts that might break.

The final reason you want to keep your items in this price range is because it allows for a lower barrier to entry into your specific market. This is due to the fact that lowered priced objects are usually economical to make in China or Thailand than higher priced items. To clarify this a little further, let's look at an example of two different products.

1. Product number one has a selling price of $24, and you can get it manufactured in China for $6 a unit. For an order of five hundred units, your order would be $3,000, not including your shipping costs.

2. Product number two has a selling price of $200, and you can get it made in China for $50 a unit. If you made an order of five hundred units, it would cost you $24,000, not including your shipping charges.

That example illustrates why you should pick a product within the selling range of ten to fifty dollars. It's much cheaper and more efficient. It also makes it easier to enter the market and business of FBA if you don't have thousands of dollars to spend on inventory.

The average selling price range is imperative to follow, and it's vital to the success of your business and product. Try to pick a product within this range if it's possible.

#2 Light

Ideally, you need a product that's as light as possible. You shouldn't get anything that's over four to five pounds because it's too heavy unless you plan on selling the product at a much higher price. When I mention weight, it refers to the shipping weight of a single unit. That includes the item, the packaging, and the shipping box.

It's impossible to know the exact weight of the product until you can get that information from the supplier. So the best way to find an estimated weight is to find a similar product on Amazon with a similar size so that you can look at their shipping weight.

For demonstrative purposes, let's say you're thinking about selling a one inch by a thirty-inch dog collar, and you need an estimate for the shipping weight. What you need to do is research a one inch by thirty-inch dog collar on Amazon and find a similar product to the one you want to sell. Scroll down until you see the product details for that item and then the shipping weight will be directly below it.

The weight is imperative because it plays a major role in the shipping cost from your supplier to Amazon's warehouse. The lighter the product is, the cheaper the shipping cost is going to be, which means a higher profit margin for you.

The weight also has a factor in the Amazon fees. Amazon will charge around two dollars for up to two pounds, and then every pound after that is another thirty-nine cents. So if your product has a weight of four pounds, then it would cost $2.78 for each unit just in the handling fees. There are also other fees that are minimized by having a light product.

Overall, the weight of the product plays a huge role in profits and the success of your item. Try to go after a light product if you can.

#3 Similar Products with a 5,000 Best Seller Rank or Lower

It's extremely hard to get a good estimate of how a certain product will sell on Amazon, but the best way to figure it out is to check out its bestseller rank.

The best seller rank tells you how well a product is selling in its category. As an example, a product with a best seller rank of twenty thousand is going to sell a lot fewer

items in the same category with a best seller
rank of 2,000.

This is useful for a seller because you can
determine if there's demand for that product in
the market or if there isn't.

You shouldn't worry about trying to sell a
product that will only sell one to two units a
day when it's sitting at number one for your
keyword. That's why it's vital to go after a
product that has demand in your market.
That's where the best seller rank comes into
play. It gives you a look at whether there's
demand for your product or not.

There are other ways you can determine the
market demand for an item, but this is the
easiest and quickest way to do it. You'll see a
few other methods later on.

There are different opinions when it comes to
bestseller rank. Some say that it has to be
below 10,000 while others say it needs to be
between 500 and 2,000. There are others who
say a product with 5,000 or below is good,
which is the median.

The more products that are below the 5,000 rank, the better. This proves there are a lot of people who are buying these products, which means that if you're in the same position as those products, then you can sell a lot, too!

So what about the main category versus the subcategory?

Just to be clear, the main category is something like Home Improvement or Pet Supplies, while the subcategory would be Table Saws or Dog Collars. You need to be more concerned with the best seller rank in the main category because a low best seller rank in the main category means its sell extremely well.

By making sure your product has other similar items that have a best seller rank below 5,000, you will ensure there are enough buyers in the market who want your product.

There are other ways you can determine market demand, but this is the best way to do it. It's also the most accurate because the data you're getting is directly from amazon.

#4 No Brand Names in Product Category or Niche

This means you don't want to compete with a brand name when you're selling your product. You want to be going up against the no-name, weak brands that carry no weight with their labeling.

The reason you want to do this is because brand dominated categories mean people will be looking at brands in order to determine which one they want to purchase. They are going to choose a brand they know over one they have never heard of before. You want the playing field to be leveled when you enter the market.

A good way to see if a brand dominates your product category is to search for the product keyword in Amazon and see if there are products that draw your attention. If you recognize a brand on the first page, then it's not a very good sign.

It's okay to see a brand on the first page if it's not exactly your product. What this means is that if you search for dog collars, and you see a bark collar that's being sold by PetSmart, then you don't need to worry too much. Bark collars aren't your market, the regular ones are. That's one example of when you see a brand on the first page it can be alright.

Ideally, you want every listing on the first page to have a different brand for each item, in addition to being a random, unknown brand.

Finding an item without a brand dominating the market is imperative because it's hard to compete with the corporate, big brands. Find a product where you are able to come in immediately and compete devoid of any disadvantages.

#5 Modest Item That Isn't Easily Broken

This is imperative.

You want to sell a product that's simple and one that you don't have to worry about arriving at the customer's home or place of business broken. The best way you can ensure a product is going to stay in one piece is to stay away from products that have more than one moving part or they're electronic.

You want to pursue items that have a single job and are generic. Some good examples might be mouse pads or yoga mats. Both have a single use, and they are generic to the point where anyone is able to get them made.

Another benefit of going after a product that's simple is you will have a much better chance of finding a manufacturer and supplier that will make the product for you. Simple merchandise going to be inexpensive to get manufactured compared to a complicated product.

Here's an easy checklist to get you started:

1. It's durable.

2. It's easily made in China.

3. There are no electronic components.

4. There are no moving components.

5. It can be used without having to have an instruction manual.

6. It's made for doing a single job.

7. It's generic.

#6 Two to Three Products with Fewer than Fifty Reviews on the First Page

This is an imperative requirement for your product due to this being a good measurement of competition.

Items that have less than fifty reviews are usually considered easy to beat. That's why you want to see at least two to three with less than fifty on the first page of results. This means there is a good chance that you can reach the first page with your product.

The more listings with fifty or fewer reviews on the first page, the better the odds you have that you will get to the first page quickly.

It's even better if there are listings that have thirty, twenty or even just five reviews. If you find a product that has a high demand and has a listing with only five reviews on the first page, then you've found yourself a product that will sell well.

The amount of reviews is one of the best ways you can gauge the level of competition when it comes to an item. You know that reviews for a product are one of core ways Amazon ranks their products. That's why you look at the number of reviews so closely before you enter the market for a product.

There are other methods you can use, but this is the easiest and quickest way when you get started.

#7 The Product is Able to be made for Twenty-Five Percent Less of Sale Price

This is the way you can quickly estimate your profit margins on a product. There's a much more exhaustive process you can experience to compute the profit margin before you make an order for a product, but this is easier.

For now, just concentrate on how to check if a product can be made for less than twenty-five percent of its sale price. How you can do this is to search for the product on a site such as Alibaba and see if the price the suppliers are making the item for is below twenty-five percent of the sale price.

Why should you do this?

You should do this check because if you can get a product made for less than twenty-five percent of its sale price, then that leaves you a seventy-five percent profit margin left over. Now, you need to remember there are shipping costs and fees to selling on amazon that will cut into this price, too.

The seventy-five percent profit margin will be plenty to cover your shipping costs and fees from amazon.

Now that you know what you have to look at before you open up your account let's get to the actual process of opening your Amazon account!

Chapter Three – Opening the Actual Amazon FBA Account

You have a product in mind, and you've done all the research, but now you need to open your actual account before you think about ordering your product. Let's go over the process in this chapter.

#1 Visit https://services.amazon.com/content/sell-on-amazon.htm

Once you've clicked on the link, you'll be taken to the page on Amazon where you can choose to register for an individual or a professional seller's account. You need to click on the *Sell as a Professional* in order to get started.

Once you've clicked on that link, you'll be taken to a page where you'll either sign in or make a new account.

#2 Either Make a New Account or Sign into an Existing Account

If you're already the proud owner of an existing Amazon account, then go ahead and use that account to sign up for your seller's account. If you don't have an Amazon account yet, then you need to make a new one. Whatever route you decide on, you'll be taken to a page where you need to input your legal name and accept the seller's agreement.

It's pretty simple. If you are based outside the United States, then you'll be shown different agreements with Amazon. Click on the continue button to go to the following step.

#3 Fill Out Seller Information

On the following page, Amazon will need to know some basic information about your brand and you. You have to fill out things like the brand name, country, address, phone number, and the type of product you'd like to sell. That's why you needed to do research beforehand. Most of the information you can fill out on your own; however, there are a few that warrant a little more discussion.

The first thing that needs to be discussed the display name. Be sure you choose your display name wisely because this is the brand you'll be selling all your products under on Amazon.

Thankfully, you're able to change this whenever you'd like. The only problem is the name you choose is not able to be taken by anyone else. Try to be sure your display name is the same as your brand name.

The second thing you should know about is the area that includes your main product category, the number of products you'd like to sell every month, and if you own the brand for the products.

Amazon states these are optional fields, but you should fill them out the best you're able. It'll only help you in the future.

When it asks if you own the brand for the items you'd like to sell, click yes. If you're private labeling an item and selling it under your brand, then you have to say yes. The people who are doing retail arbitrage are going to be the ones who say no, but you're not going to do that.

#4 Add Credit Card Information

On the following page, you'll be asked to input your credit or debit card information. You have to do this because Amazon will charge this card for your monthly fee for having the professional seller's account. They are also going to use this card to verify your identity.

#5 Verify Identity

Even though Amazon is going to use your credit card in order to verify your identity, you will need to do a phone verification. You can do this through text or through an actual phone call.

This is easy and will only take a few minutes to complete.

#6 Tax Information

The final step to setting up the account is being sure Amazon has all your right tax records. They make this process simple with their Tax Interview Wizard, which will walk you through the entire process.

Once you click on the Launch Interview Wizard, you'll be brought to the start of the interview. Don't worry, this is not a live interview. Once you click on that, you'll be taken to another page.

Just follow the instructions on the screen and you should be golden. Once you click continue, you'll be brought to a page where you will need to tell Amazon how you'd like to be taxed.

You should create a Limited Liability Company in your state and use that for selling on Amazon. There are many reasons for this.

If you already have an LLC set up for Amazon, then choose the option and choose that option and then choose the S-Corporation. Fill out your EIN number at the bottom, along with the remaining information and then you can keep going to the following page.

The following two pages will need to be filled out and then signed electronically.

#7 You're Ready!

After you complete the tax interview, then you're finished setting up the account! Now you have an Amazon professional seller's account, and you're ready to begin selling on Amazon.

You have your research, and you have your seller's account, so you can go ahead and begin ordering your inventory. It can take anywhere from one month to a few months in order to get your first set of inventory to Amazon, so you want to get the processed started as soon as possible.

You can do this by contacting the manufacturer you want to use and ordering from them. We'll learn more about that in the following chapter.

Chapter Four – Tips for Ordering from Suppliers

The most popular supplier out there for people who are selling through FBA is Alibaba. However, there are other platforms you can take a look at. No matter who you decide to order from, here are some ways you can make sure the process goes smoothly.

#1 Never Assume

When it comes to ordering from a vendor, you should never make an assumption about the availability of your product. On many occasions, there have been times where a

vendor tried to sell a product that wasn't displayed on their site. In addition, you should always request samples of products that are not displayed on their site.

A vendor's website is often not up to date, and some are better than others at maintaining online offerings. Therefore, be communicative with vendors about what you want, whether it's displayed or not on their site.

#2 Don't be Intimidated

Most vendors will respond in a quick and friendly fashion, which reinforces the importance of building a relationship with them. While, in a few instances, a vendor may seem cold, most are eager to engage in conversation and answer questions.

For the most part, their written English is excellent. Their ability to send and receive e-mails is very effective, so don't be afraid to jump right into a conversation with them.

#3 Trust Your Instincts

Some vendors are a little too friendly. That's probably due to some cultural differences, but when they send you two to three emails a day asking if you'd like to buy something and you've said no three to four times, then it's time to worry a little. There are spammers everywhere, so just be aware of who you're speaking with and trust your instincts.

#4 Be Specific

Tailor your inquiries for each vendor for the specific product category you're interested in.

It seems obvious, but it's imperative to be specific from the get-go about what you want to purchase, including types, materials, color, size, and more.

#5 You Might Not Get What You Expect

Despite doing all of the suggested tips up until this point, there are some occasions where you get samples that were not what you ordered. When you confront the vendor, the typical answer will be they only had that one available for shipment or that the product was discontinued. You are not going to get a second chance to make an impression, so hold the vendors who do this accountable.

#6 Most Vendors Expect a Wire Transfer

Most vendors are going to let you pay through PayPal. Some will have PayPal but will not let you know unless you ask them to be sure. In fact, with most of them will require that a sample purchase is made through PayPal.

While most will accept purchases through PayPal, they are definitely going to prefer a default wire transfer.

#7 Always Get Samples

Samples are an investment in the final product. While purchasing samples might seem like a daunting task, be sure you keep it in perspective. Compared to an initial investment, the risk to reward ratio is much greater for an online store, not to mention the difference in lifestyle. Don't be afraid to spend a little money on samples.

#8 Act Bigger Than You Really Are

Use 'we' rather than 'I' and 'our' instead of 'my'. This makes your company appear larger than it really is, and it also displays a sense of unity and teamwork.

#9 Know the Difference between a Manufacturer and Trading Company

In general, it's easy to tell if a supplier is a trading company or a manufacturer, but there are some trends between the trading companies and manufacturers.

Usually, companies that say 'Import/Export Co' are usually not manufacturers even if their company profile states they are. Along with obvious things such as MOQ and price differences, trading companies have a pushier sales approach while the manufacturer wants to build a relationship with you.

Know who you are dealing with when it comes to supplier sand the pros and cons of working with a trading company versus a manufacturer.

#10 Be Prepared When Shipping

Most vendors are going to set up the shipping for you, and all you need to do is provide them with a phone number and shipping address for confirmation purposes. Just know that it's going to cost you a ton, and the shipping can cost you more than the actual samples. It's a good idea to confirm shipping costs before you pay for samples.

Now that you know some of the tips on handling ordering from a manufacturer let's look at how to boost your sales with advertising!

Chapter Five – Boosting Sales with Advertising

Ideally, you want a product that will sell itself as much as possible, but if you want to boost sales in the beginning to get your listing up there, you need to advertise. Advertising comes in two forms, free and not free. We'll take a look at both forms in this chapter.

Facebook

Facebook is a site that many people are familiar with. Once of the best ways to sell products you are selling on Amazon is to be active on Facebook. Connecting with fans, sharing news, persuading fans to share information, and hosting competitions are all ways to get your product out in the public's line of sight. This is usually more time-consuming, and you have to keep at it in order to see a significant increase in sales, but it will work if you put the time and effort into it.

Twitter

Twitter is another highly popular social media site that you can use in order to increase sales and promote your items. Once you have many followers, you have people who will be interested in your brand and products, and you can promote new products or information directly to this audience. If they enjoy what they are seeing, then there's a good chance they will share this information with their followers. Similar to Facebook, Twitter requires you put some time and effort into it in order to see a good return rate. You also need to be sure you evade being too self-promotional so you don't annoy followers.

Pinterest

This is a relatively new platform that has gained extreme popularity in the past few years. The entire platform enables a user to make a theme that's focused on boards where they can pin images from all over the web. When you consider the ease of making a new pin and the extreme number of people who use and are willing to re-pin posts they like, it's excellent for exposing your items and website to an entirely new crowd. The platform is totally free, and it's easy to setup, which means it's worth regularly posting on it, even if you don't see much from it initially. It only takes a few people to re-pin your pins in order to get a decent level of traffic.

Daily Deals

There are many daily deal sites that are around anymore, and the most notable ones are Living Social and Groupon. These sites are centered on offering purchasers excellent deals on products, holidays, and gifts based on a certain number of people who are purchasing them. If companies choose to use this platform for promotion, they can make a lot of sales in a short period of time, and they can increase the awareness of their brand.

There is a good chance that these people will return to purchase again after they have used the daily deal. It's worth noting that there are times where people underestimate the number of sales that are able to be achieved through these platforms and have found they are in a position where they cannot fulfill orders, so be careful.

Landing Pages and PPC

PPC or Pay per Click offers you a guaranteed way to get visitors to your site. It ensures you have full control over how much money you spend and if you have a rough idea of the percentage of visitors that convert when they visit your website, you can be sure you always have a profit. By combining an optimized Pay per Click campaign with a targeted landing page, you can be sure that every visitor will be interested in the product you're selling. TI's then down to the landing page to convince them to purchase this product.

Email

E-mail is considered old technology when it's compared to the other options on the internet, but it's still an excellent way to build awareness of a new product to an existing or a new customer. Usually, of someone has agreed to sign up for an e-mail from you, they are already attracted to the products you have to offer. This gives you the chance to entice them with a special offer or highlight products to them that they might enjoy.

Reviews

Reviews will help send traffic to your product, and they can persuade someone to make a purchase once they've arrived at your product page. There are many ways where reviews can be used for your benefit. First, you can be sure you are listed on as many external review sites as you can so that customers can find you if they want to comment on a good experience. Some examples might be Review Centre and The Best Of. This can help send visitors to your product page if people are using these platforms.

You can also display reviews on a business website to help improve the amount of sales you are likely to achieve. People are a lot more likely to purchase an item if they can see others have previously used the site, and they have been happy with their purchases. If you have a number of excellent reviews on your website or an external website, then you can draw attention to them using Rich Snippets. This displays the average rating in the search results and helps encourage searchers to click through to your site.

Product Videos

Lastly, the power of videos is still very underestimated. There's a huge audience on sites such as YouTube and other platforms where potential customers are likely to search for a product and its related reviews. If you make some informative, well thought out videos of high quality, then you can capture the attention of an audience that previously might not have discovered you.

Now that you know how to boost sales let's take a look at why you should try Amazon FBA.

Chapter Six – Why Should You Try It?

You've most likely discovered some benefits already throughout this book, but there are some specifics we should go over if you're not completely convinced yet. Let's take a look at them!

#1 Access Prime Subscribers

Prime subscribers are those who pay a set fee every year to Amazon in order to access items that can be shipped to them within two days for free. You can't ask for a better customer than that!

Prime subscribers are loyal to Amazon, and they also purchase more expensive items and purchase 150% more than a non-Prime customer. They spend around $1,340 on Amazon every year, where a non-Prime customer will pay just $529a year.

Selling with FBA will give you access to a larger customer base. Specific numbers are not released by Amazon, but there are an estimated fifty million Prime subscribers, which is a huge customer base!

#2 You Don't Have to Handle Shipping, Customer Service, and Returns

When a sale has been made, Amazon will pick it out of their warehouse, pack it, and ship it to the customer. Quick shipping will make a customer happy, and a happy customer is someone who will be more likely to purchase your exact product again in the future.

If your customer is not satisfied with their service, Amazon will handle that, as well. This will save you time and money because there isn't a need for you to employ customer service representatives.

Lastly, due to items being stored in Amazon's warehouses, you don't have to worry about needing all that inventory space for your products.

#3 FBA's a Tiebreaker in the Buy Box

Depending on your product's category, you can price up to around two to ten percent higher than competitors and still get the Buy Box if you use FBA and competitors are not. That's due to shipping being factored into the total cost.

#4 Higher Sales Volume

While it's not guaranteed, most sellers see a twenty percent or more sales volume when they switch to Fulfillment by Amazon. Many sellers report even higher sales jumps, including double what they originally sold!

#5 customers are willing to Pay More

The millions of Prime subscribers out there know a good deal when they see one. You can factor the cost of shipping into your price, and Prime customers are willing to sacrifice a few dollars in order to ensure they receive their product in two days.

So you see, it's well worth it to become a seller using FBA.

Chapter Seven – Tips for Staying Organized

So you've decided to become an Amazon seller using FBA, and you have your products listed and selling, but what about staying organized? The key difference between successful sellers using FBA and those who fail within the first few months is organization. Here are some tips that will help you stay successful!

#1 Supplier Relationships

Let's take a look at two different scenarios. One is where your main provider cuts you off from retailing the brand on Amazon, and the other is where the merchant offers you the exclusive opportunity to sell on Amazon. What impacts those two scenarios? Communication does. It's the key difference between a successful FBA seller and a mediocre seller.

An elite FBA seller has an excellent relationship with their supplier and, as a result, they open doors for VIP treatment and other prospects that make for a more competitive advantage over their competitors.

As someone who opens a business, your highest Return on Investment or ROI activity is building the supply chain and the relationships with the manufacturers. It's easy to feel there isn't any time amid purchase orders, shipping, and your other daily tasks, but investing in the supplier and becoming their best customer puts you higher up on their list when it comes to competitors. In the internet-focused world, people forget about building relationships, but I can't stress enough the importance of trade shows, in-person meetings, and other events that will help you network and grow your business relationships.

The key element here is a mutually beneficial relationship in order to negotiate opportunity with manufacturers and suppliers.

#2 Your Purchasing Process

Are you the owner of the business and the primary buyer or do you have a team? A single person who is handling an entire folder full of SKUs is not a scalable business model. Instead, you need some organized management of a financially driven buying team. When you build a buying team, you allow yourself to build a performance-based system that's focused on quantity and quality that increases the number of Fulfillment by Amazon investments without sacrificing your performance and depth. This gives you infinite opportunities to scale your relationship and brands, without spreading yourself out too thin.

When you build a team, it's imperative to hire traders and not retail buyers. People who are focused on data are going to succeed on Amazon because it's a trading platform with a different mindset than that of a traditional retail buyer. And a team that is data-focused is trackable each step of the way. You have to constantly track and report their performance.

You should also create some healthy competition between the team. What gets measured should also be managed, and along with constant performance measurements comes the necessity for management and adjustments. Incentives will help motivate success in your team.

#3 Growth Strategy

The most common mistake seen in scaling a Fulfillment by Amazon company is that more brands equal rapid growth. Adding as many brands as you can is not going to build you a profitable Fulfillment by Amazon business.

Elite Fulfillment by Amazon retailers are obsessive about the maximization o the most valuable product opportunities they have, as opposed to the amount of brands they have. Even if you don't have an automation process, there are numbers you need to know. It can take some time in Excel or another spreadsheet software, but it's necessary to track investments and prioritize the highest opportunities first.

When you track these investments, you focus on letting a computer facilitate formative thinking that allows humans and computers to work together to make a decision and control a complex situation. Computers should do about eighty percent of the work while people do the other twenty percent.

Numbers are only going to get you so far, and it always will take an educated human to take a look at data and make a decision. Let the program do the weighty work when recognizing venture opportunities, but remember the significance of the buying team to examine that data and finalize the decision-making process.

#4 Stale Inventory Control

This is the silent killer of any Fulfillment by Amazon business. You might not be on top of your old inventory on a periodic schedule. You might be sporadically cleaning it up and being sure to stay on top of some long-term deadlines. But that's not all you have to do.

A successful Fulfillment by Amazon business is going to monitor stale inventory consistently and focus on turning it over and exiting out of a stale investment. Consistently means on a weekly and daily basis. It might seem easier to focus your attention on new brands and new inventory because it's easy to spend money, especially if you believe it will help the business. However, you could be spending money you don't really have because it's tied up in the stale inventory you've been ignoring.

Nobody wants to handle stale inventory. Your supplier is not going to give you advice on these investments, and they are not going to tell you to stop purchasing items that are not selling. It's up to you to manage stale inventory. You should work obsessively on figuring out what's hurting your business on an everyday basis and make a controlled approach to exiting out of those poor investments.

#5 Investment Strategy

Because you've started a retail business, you have some capital. However, the huge question is where is that capital? Have you spread it out across a large portfolio, tying it up in some long-term investments? Or did you identify those short windows of opportunity to cycle your capital quickly? Hopefully, you're in the latter group, and you have the knowledge and tools to generate profit from one investment.

Look at investments as a never-ending cycle.

Now that you know how to stay organized let's take a look at expansion more closely.

Chapter Eight – Expansion

So you've stayed organized, and your business is taking off, but how do you expand? How do you go from being someone who does this part time to someone who can fully rely on their FBA sales for their full-time income?

#1 Work on Your Strengths

Are you passionate about what you sell? Do you have the resources and connections in your industry in order to leverage and expand your business? One way you can ensure you continue to build and keep interest in the business over the long-term is to sell a product you're really excited and passionate about!

Hiring is another factor entirely. When you hire, actively seek out those who share a similar passion. A qualified team will help you grow your business a lot faster than you could accomplish alone.

Lastly, don't forget to build that relationship with the supplier. Check to see if the company is willing to help reduce costs or improve the quality of your products. Communicate that you're in this for the long-term. If this company is not willing to listen to requests, you might want to find a new manufacturer.

#2 Track and Record Numbers

As a Fulfillment by Amazon owner, you need to record and track your financial numbers from the first day. This lets you keep an eye on the lifeblood of the business, and if you want to sell that online business in the future, this data is going to be invaluable to you. Record more data than you think you will ever need, and set up some redundancies for accuracy.

In addition, keep a close eye on the cost efficiency of the business. Are you profitable after all the fees and expenses are accounted for? In most cases, a Fulfillment by Amazon business will see an adjusted gross margin of fifteen to twenty percent. How does your current business compare?

Many business owners won't ask themselves these questions when they start a Fulfillment by Amazon business. IN order to manage your cash flow, you should track key performance indicators, such as your inventory turn rates, inventory to sales ratios, cash to cash cycle, gross margin return on investment, and days of inventory.

#3 Extend Online Presence with a Website

The problem with using Amazon as a business platform is that you don't own it!

This means you don't have access to customer data, which is a complication because if you'd like to build and scale your business over the long-term, this information is critical to success.

There are tools you can use to gain access to this information, but it's also a good move to develop and establish a business website to get some of your own data. There are benefits to building your own online presence with a website.

First, you can direct some customer traffic to your site while you still build awareness for your brand and products. Web sites are also an excellent place to begin collection e-mail addresses. When you do this, you can begin sending out targeted e-mails, sharing news about promotions, and announcing new products to subscribers and past customers.

In addition, note that you own the e-mail list that you build. This is an invaluable asset, especially if you're thinking about selling the business in the future.

#4 Use Paid Advertising

Search engine optimization is a long-term strategy, and because you can't start optimizing a site that you don't own beyond the product information supplied by you, paid advertising is an accessible way to promote your product without having to make small tweaks to your website and building huge amounts of content. It's possible you can reduce customer acquisition costs by up to eighty percent when you use advertising.

In order to be successful in advertising, you need to be prepared for a lot of trial and error. No matter how well you believe you know your business, you might not immediately land a winning strategy. To get the most out of ad campaigns, you need to:

1. Considering use two different images to test which ones your target customers engage with the most. People are going to see the image first and then read the copy.

2. Split test the copy. Just like with images, you might be discovered that the kind of print that echoes with your purchaser is different than you thought.

3. Gather some audience information. Build the e-mail list on the website, and use tools such as Amazon MWS Customer/Order Export service to comprehend your audience and build some look-alike audiences you can advertise to.

4. Use retargeting. This means capturing buyers off-site before they disappear forever.

#5 Improve Best-Seller Rank

There isn't really a step-by-step guide for optimizing the Best Seller Rank. Rather, the common belief is that the Best Seller Rank consists of historical and recent sales combined.

Yet, best seller rank is an imperative measurement and one that you need to focus on improving. The primary means is to outsell the competition. If this is challenging for you, then keep in mind it's always possible to change your product offering to go into a less competitive category.

Customer reviews and ratings are also going to factor into your overall best seller ranking. Be sure you offer your customers the best products and services you can in order to avoid negative ratings and reviews.

Conclusion

Fulfillment by Amazon is definitely an excellent business model to get started with if you're not familiar with the retail industry. You can easily build brand recognition on this platform and even branch out to building your own website and advertising on more expensive platforms once you've gained some capital in your business. The best part about this business model is that there are a minimal investment and a minimal risk, so if you don't end up picking a product that sells well, you can always try again!

Remember, you need to choose products that are already selling well if you want your first venture to do well, too.

I hope you enjoyed the information you found in this book and found it helpful! If so, please leave a review at your online eBook retailer's website.

Thank you for reading!

BEFORE YOU GO

If you liked this book you may like these other books from Mark Thomas

Check out more books by Mark Thomas

Free Bonus

As Promised Here Is Your Guide To
Creating More Hours In Your Day:
Discover How To Fit 48 Hours Of Work
In A Day

GET YOUR FREE COPY

LEARN HOW TO GET MORE DONE IN A DAY

Do you feel stuck, stressed, and pissed because you aren't able to get all of your most important tasks done in a day? Perhaps this book can be the answer to your struggles. Learn the ways to manage your time to get more things done in a day and free up time do things you enjoy in life. Procrastination and Distractions are the biggest enemy of time management. This book will teach you the exact strategies to conquer procrastination.

Download "The Clockwork Course" For FREE

If You Want Free Best Selling Kindle Books Delivered Straight To Your Inbox

JOIN OUR FREE KINDLE BOOK CLUB!

BE PART OF THE CLUB

Chapter One – The Money Mindset

Before you even begin to think about making over ten thousand dollars in a month in just ninety days, you have to know what the proper mindset is in order to achieve that goal. You see, your mindset is extremely important to what you want to achieve. If you tell yourself you can't do something, then you won't be able to achieve it! So let's explore how you can have the proper money mindset in order to get rich!

First, let's take a look at an example of someone who has a money mindset and someone who doesn't. We'll take a look at two handymen. Handyman one, let's call him George, walks into a home and he is approached by the homeowner. The homeowner tells him or her they want crown molding put in their upstairs bathroom. George affably agrees it will make the appearance of their home nicer, but that's it.

Now, the second handyman's name is Josh. Josh walks into the home and he approaches the homeowner who tells him about wanting the crown molding. Josh also agrees it will look nicer, but he also goes on to explain how the crown molding will improve the value of the home over the long run.

Do you see the difference? George just wanted to make the home look better for aesthetic purpose only, but Josh saw the *value* in putting the crown molding in from an investment standpoint.

Being able to see the value in something is the money mindset. There are numerous other aspects to the money mindset, so let's take a look at them.

#1 Mindful of the Long-Term

There are many people out there who are looking to make money fast, but they rarely ever make a lot of it because of greed. Their first mindset is to think about what's in it for them. Rather, they should be thinking about how they can add as much value to someone else first. For example, it's like building credits with someone or an organization over the long-term. You might never need to use those credits, but if you do, help is returned in abundance. Don't allow your short-term greed destroy your long-term wealth.

#2 You Deserve Only What You've Earned

There is no room for an attitude of entitlement for someone when they have a money mindset. Don't expect to get to the corner office without paying your dues. At sixty-three years old, the man who put up the crown moldings is a great example of someone who doesn't expect something. He comes in with a good attitude to his job, does it well, cleans up, and leaves.

#3 You Believe You Deserve to be Wealthy

Money is out there for anyone to get their hands on. Once you believe you deserve to have that money, you'll subconsciously change your actions to make it happen. Stop feeling guilty about earning six figures in a year. There are people out there who earn seven and drive their companies into the ground to do it! Your mindset should not be 'why me' but 'why *not* me'? With the belief that you deserve to be wealthy too, your income will soar!

#4 You Ask Yourself What the Value of The Product or Service is Before You Spend a Dollar

People who have the money mindset are very value aware. Since they realize how hard it is to make money, they are much more careful about spending their money than the average person. They have to ask whether one dollar spent might return that dollar in the future. They are on the lookout for great deals and tend not to feel buyer's remorse because they purchase things that have a greater value than what they paid.

#5 You're Always Looking for Synergies and Leverage

When you go out to play tennis with people at a club or you're hanging out with some new friends, get excited! There could be synergies involved with those people. Not only are you having a good time with those people, but you are parlaying your relationship right into an excellent business opportunity. A website is an excellent example of leveraging assets to earn more. Besides earning advertising money, you can earn money by selling products and services. Your website can also serve as an online resume PR hub if you want to do more public works. If you haven't started a website, you really ought to!

#6 You Realize a Dollar Spent Today Could Grow To Much More In The Future

People who have the money mindset are naturally frugal. They despise letting go of too much money because they've already figured out what they spent today might have turned into if they had saved and invested at a ten percent rate of return over the following five to thirty years. Compound growth anchors money mindset people into spending less than they have earned. With an aggressive savings rate, you'll be surprised with just how much you could accumulate in a 401k in ten years.

#7 You're All About Tax Optimization

It's imperative to think about how much you have to earn before purchasing a particular item due to taxes. A car that costs $21,000 requires you to actually earn $30,000 in gross income. In terms of making money, someone who has a money mindset will look to reduce their taxes by figuring out the most tax friendly way they can make money passively, such as dividends. They also look to synergize their expenses if they are a freelancer or small business. There's no reason to do a company offsite in North Dakota if you can do one in Kauai. Figuring out how to pay little or no taxes becomes a hobby for someone with a money mindset.

#8 You Believe Excuses are No Excuse

You're either going to make it happen or you're going to fail. Failure is just fine; just don't make excuses and not do something about it. Figure out the reasons why you failed and then try again until you succeed. You need to believe you deserve only what you've earned, you take ownership for your failures and you most past them. Excuses are for those who blame the world for their shortcomings rather than themselves. The more excuses you use, the less you believe you are able to make things happen on your own.

#9 You Never Fail Due to a Lack of Effort

You can fail because your competition is incredibly talented, there was bad timing, or a natural disaster happened, but you will never fail due to a lack of doing your best. There are many people out there who say they are going to make a living writing or freelance programming, but most of them won't even send a draft of what they're writing to someone else for feedback. They don't want to put in the time to make the money.

#10 You Execute Solutions

Recognizing a problem or coming up with an idea is one thing. Coming up with the solution is more important. There are so many people out there who like to point out injustices or complain about something, but none of them doing anything about the situation. Someone with the money mindset will find a way to get it done and make it better.

If you read through this chapter and you believe you don't have the money mindset, don't despair! Anyone can develop the money mindset. The first step is to know you're worth it and believing that you deserve to be wealthy. If you put in the effort, there is no reason you can't be enjoying that passive income flow, too.

Now that you know what the money mindset is and you know where you have to change in order to become wealthy with passive income let's look at the amazing ways you can make ten thousand dollars in a month in just ninety days!

Chapter Two – Making Money as a Coach

Are you currently struggling to make money with your coaching business but you have an expectation to make ten thousand dollars a month? Stop struggling! It's absolutely possible to make six figures a year coaching business, and it can happen pretty fast if you follow the necessary steps you need in order to fill your e-mail list and focus on getting more calls.

These are the top tips for making ten thousand dollars a month or more in as little as ninety days. That doesn't mean it's going to happen overnight easily. Building a business takes some focus and some effort. The goal is to build relationships and help the ideal client solve specific problems they're facing, and you're the coach and mentor that can help them with the problem.

The first step is developing that money mindset. Having the right mindset is extremely important when it comes to almost anything in your life. Making a consistent ten thousand dollars a month is not an exception.

You can create a vision board in order to visualize your goal. Just cut out some pictures and words from a favorite magazine and add them to a pinboard. You can also create an online one with Pinterest that's private and filled with inspiring images and quotes!

Once you've developed the mindset, you need to test those coaching packages.

Test the Packages

Market research is the core principle of making a thriving coaching package and coaching business. Don't make a package you believe will sell. Create a package based off what your ideal client actually desires.

In the first module of testing your packages, you need to ask detailed questions of your target market to be sure you are going to make packages that will actually sell. Don't skip this step! Make your market research your priority.

If you already have packages that are not selling, then find out why. Ask the ideal client what they would like to see added to the package or if there is anything else you can help them with. Change your copywriting in order to put an emphasis on the benefits and allow the readers know exactly what they can expect to occur if they work with you.

Price the Packages

In order to bring your income goals to life, you need to price your services and packages accordingly. Many coaches undercharge for their services. But if you want to be someone who goes to exotic locations and has financial freedom, then you need to create a premium coaching package!

Perhaps the thought of charging more for your package frightens you. If this is the case, keep working on your money mindset and remind yourself that your services are worth it for your clients.

Making a good income from what you do for a living will help you not only have a happy, healthy life, but it will help you be of a greater service to your clients. You'll have more income you can invest in your education as a coach, which will help you keep enhancing your skills.

Here are the following action steps you should follow in this section:

1. Figure out how many of your current coaching packages you have to sell in order for you to make the ten thousand dollars a month.

2. Ask yourself if you are undercharging. If you are, increase your rates and make new packages.

3. Work on your money mindset and beliefs if you are bumping against statements like *I can't charge that much*. It's not your packages that are the problem, it's you.

Lead Generation

Ads are an excellent way to generate leads. In fact, they're so important when it comes to growing a coaching business that they are one of the essential keys to financial freedom! Try some Facebook or Google ads for your coaching business and you'll see it increase.

There are other ways you can generate leads, too, such as going through a guest post, doing a webinar, joint ventures, and teleclasses.

Whatever you choose to begin with, keeping going with it! Make sure to keep your efforts going so that your list grows with those are interested in getting to know you and the services you provide.

Here are the actions steps that will lead you to success!

1. Create some sort of lead generating strategy. How many leads to you require coming in so that you can hit ten thousand dollars a month? How many discovery or strategy sessions do you need to have to sign the number of clients you need in order to result in ten thousand dollars a month?

2. Invest time and learning in how to run Facebook ads or pay an expert to set them up for you.

3. Read and post on how to do a webinar.

4. Begin using Facebook ads or Google ads to promote your first webinar or opt-in gift.

Consistent Marketing

A successful coach will not flip-flop when it comes to their business. They will be consistent in marketing and expanding their reach. Ask yourself how consistent you are with marketing when it comes to your business. Are you in touch with your e-mail subscribers on a regular basis? What can your readers expect from a blog or newsletter? How do your readers feel about your brand and what are they learning from you?

Consistent marketing and lead generation helps you obtain more clients and hit your ten thousand dollar a month income. It's not rocket science. It's a formula that successful coaches and marketers have been following for some time.

Here are your action steps for continuous marketing.

1. Consider hiring a virtual assistant or hiring and intern for a few hours a week so you can focus on client generation activities.

2. Focus on some money making activities, such as getting leads, booking discovery calls, marketing, and much more. E-mail your list of contacts three times a week with one newsletter and two solo e-mails. Solo e-mails are the ones you send out that have a single call to action. It usually has something to do with income generation.

<u>Check out more books by Mark Thomas</u>

Thank you again for downloading this book!

If you enjoyed this book, then I'd like to ask you for a favor, would you be kind enough to leave a review for this book on Amazon? It'd be greatly appreciated!

Thank you and good luck! ☺

-Mark Thomas